Darkening Water

Books by Daniel Hoffman

POETRY

Middens of the Tribe
Hang-Gliding from Helicon: New and Selected Poems
Brotherly Love
The Center of Attention
Broken Laws
Striking the Stones
A Little Geste
An Armada of Thirty Whales

TRANSLATION

A Play of Mirrors, by Ruth Domino

PROSE

Zone of the Interior: A Memoir, 1942–1947
Words to Create a World: Essays, Interviews, and Reviews of Contemporary Poetry
Faulkner's Country Matters
Poe Poe Poe Poe Poe Poe Poe
Barbarous Knowledge: Myth in the Poetry of Yeats, Graves, and Muir
Form and Fable in American Fiction
The Poetry of Stephen Crane
Paul Bunyan, Last of the Frontier Demigods

AS EDITOR

Ezra Pound and William Carlos Williams
Harvard Guide to Contemporary American Writing
American Poetry and Poetics
The Red Badge of Courage and Other Tales

poems

Darkening Water

DANIEL HOFFMAN

Louisiana State University Press Baton Rouge
2002

Manufactured in the United States of America
First printing
11 10 09 08 07 06 05 04 03 02
5 4 3 2 1

Designer: Barbara Neely Bourgoyne
Typeface: Bembo
Printer and binder: Thomson-Shore, Inc.

Library of Congress Cataloging-in-Publication Data

Hoffman, Daniel, 1923–
Darkening water : poems / Daniel Hoffman.
p. cm.
ISBN 0-8071-2771-X (Hardcover : alk. paper)—ISBN 0-8071-2772-8 (Paperback : alk. paper)
I. Title.
PS3515.O2416 D37 2002
811'.54—dc21

2001005192

The paper in this book meets the guidelines for permanence and durability of the Committee on Production Guidelines for Book Longevity of the Council on Library Resources. ♾

Various poems first appeared, sometimes in slightly different form, as follows:

Atlanta Review: "A Rose d'Isfahan in Maine"; *Beloit Poetry Journal:* "Speech"; *Boulevard:* "Summer" (titled "August"), "Identities," "Quandaries," "Vane,"; *Critical Quarterly* (England): "Emblems"; *The Dark Horse* (Scotland): "Heartbreak"; *Georgia Review:* "O Pioneers!" and "Scott Nearing's Ninety-Eighth Year"; *Gettysburg Review:* "Treasure," "A Wall of Stone," "A Pile of Rocks," "Going," and "A Witness"; *Grand Street:* "Who We Are"; *Hudson Review:* "Blizzard," "On First Looking into Lattimore's Homer," "Mean Street," "Bob," and "Called Back"; *Kentucky Review:* "At the Lookout" (in an issue dedicated to Dabney Stuart); *One Trick Pony:* "Near Tinicum Island"; *Poetry:* "Fables"; *Shenandoah:* "The Gift of Tongues" (titled "End of a Tradition"); *Yale Review:* "Evidence."

"Ballad of the Day" in *New Directions 43* (New York: New Directions, 1981); "Going" in *Pushcart Prize XXV* (2001); "Identities" in *The Best American Poetry, 1992,* edited by Charles Simic (New York: Macmillan, 1992); "Ledges" in *Winslow Homer and the Sea,* by Carl Little (San Francisco: Pomegranate Art Books, 1995); "Saturday" in *Sometime the Cow Kicks Your Head: Light Year '88/9,* edited by Robert Wallace (Cleveland: Bits Press, 1988); "Vane" as a Turret Bookshop Broadside (London, 1993); "Violence" in *The Road to Parnassus; Homage to Peter Russell on His Seventy-fifth Birthday,* edited by James Hogg (Salzburg; University of Salzburg, 1996); and "Who We Are" in *The Best American Poetry, 1991,* edited by Mark Strand (New York: Macmillan, 1991).

"In the Gallery," "The Cape Racer," and "Devotion" were originally published in *The New Yorker.*

Contents

1

Summer

This busy day has poured on the horizon
A molten sky that cools,
Crystallizing into stars.

And these rocks with their smooth breasts,
Their dark mouths, exhale a fading
Warmth hoarded from memory of the sun.

A breeze tentatively comes from somewhere
Far at sea, searching for a lover,
For bestowal, bringing its caresses,

Bringing words etched on this page,
A white prow I launch now
To cleave the darkening water.

Identities

One searches roads receding, endlessly receding.
The other opens all the doors with the same key. Simple.

One's quick to wrath, the wronged, the righteous, the wroth
kettledrum.
The other loafs by the river, idles and jiggles his line.

One conspires against statues on stilts, in his pocket
The plot that dooms the city. The other's a *good* son.

One proclaims he aims to put the first aardvark in space.
The other patiently toils to make saddles for horseless headmen.

One exults as he flexes the glees of his body, up-down, up-down.
The other's hawk-kite would sail, would soar—who has tied it to
carrion and bones?

One's a Tom Fool about money—those are his pockets, those with
the holes.
At his touch, gold reverts to the base living substance.

The other's a genius, his holdings increase by binary fission—
Ownings beget their own earnings, dividend without end.

One clasps in a bundle and keens for the broken ten laws.
The other scratches in Ogham the covenant of a moral pagan.

One with alacrity answers to "121-45-3628?"—"Yes, *sir!*" The other
Bends his knee, doffs cap to no man living or dead. One

Does all his doings as ordained by diskette or disk,
The other draws his dreams through the eye of the moon.

In the Gallery

Here neither nymph nor naiad ever bathed
nor saint refreshed herself in pristine water,

here, in The Gallery, between Tie Rack,
Camera Shop, B. Dalton, Radio Shack,

Dad's Pizzas, Software, Message Cards, and Chez
Chocolat, a stream and pool's contained

by marble, or simulated marble, banks
with fountains on two levels and a water-

fall—the pumped recycled water's
splash and gurgles cool or seem to cool

the loud bright air so filled with crowds and hawkers,
bottom agleam with shining coins whose shimmer

reflects the neon clash of colors flashing
on pennies aglitter, gleaming quarters, dimes

tossed in from the concrete shores or flung
from the arched bridge that joins one aisle

of bargains to the other, each coin thrown
with a silent, urgent wish to some power unseen—

Dear Goddess of Good Luck, whatever your name now,
please smile on us, who make this place your grove.

Treasure

Buried gold of my inmost distress
—Will it be always hid from me? I hold

Between my palms a forked divining rod,
And as I trudge on littered roads

Through the countries of one day
And another day, past empty houses,

Their abandoned banquets gnawed by mice,
Where the musicians left without their pay,

The lovers vanished, the children gone,
The wise branch in my hands points down

Toward bulging sacks deep underground
Swelling with plenty, each night richer

Than before. Here's ransom for the king
Of the final country—he'll set free

The captive trumpeters, the missing lovers,
Children banished from their playthings,

And all lost years will be redeemed.

Evidence

On sandy floor, the evidence: thighbone, ribs,
skulls of antelope and deer, ringed by pawprints;
scuffed beside the circle of ashes, toeprints
and sticks with one end burnt, left where they'd been thrown
before some quake or ancient avalanche had
sealed this cavern—how many millennia
ago we cannot know till spectroscopic
test results come in on sample sticks and bones.
But we infer that this is where it happened:
The titan immemorial sabretooth
roaring his outrage, all defiance baffled
by wavering lights, by hot brands thrust or thrown
from his own cave's mouth where, erect and shaggy,
two creatures shout before the living, crackling
flames. A-dance on cavern wall, the quick shadow
of woman crouched at fireside, one hand holding
her swelling belly, the other clutching, closed
between her legs, the lid soon to be bursting
open. She yells encouragement to her mate
and his clever brother who, when lightning struck
the dead oak, with his flint hacked hot punk onto
a flat stone, and brought the smouldering ashes here.

A Rose d'Isfahan in Maine

You can cut turf in the grown-over
weedy dooryard
of the old farmhouse by the bay,

turn up a crop of buried stones,
then snug down
the tendril roots of your shrub rose,

sod it in, pour on the necessary
bucket of water.
Good luck. Neither your rose's pedigree

from the arms of a Norman duchess
and, before her,
the pleasure garden of a prince of Persia,

nor its portraits, minuscule on vellum
or by Gobelin
prinked with stitches, will impress the weather.

Leave it to the wind's ministrations,
to fog as cool
as a seal's breath, and the intermittent

skillet of the sun. So may it thrive with yarrow,
uncouth dogbane,
and milky ways of daisies in the rumpled meadow.

A Wall of Stone

The way granite tugs, tugs the arms,
the back that strains to lift it, the way
granite hugs the earth,
the way it catches glints of sun
—white fireflecks in mica specks
set in the gray black-dotted glow
of granite—the way these rough-cut blocks
push down on one another
till one's bulges nudge another's
hollows, once set beneath, beside,
atop each other, determined not
to budge, the way
behind these rows of roses
and phlox this drywall rises
as granite pulls the heat
out of the air all morning, all
the afternoon, slowly
giving back at evening, the way
holding sea-winds at bay the granite
shields and encloses phlox
and roses so you'd say these giddy
fragrances are blown
from the warm blocks of the gray stone.

A Pile of Rocks

Wading waist-deep through hardhack, daisies, yarrow,
In a fringe of ferns at the foot of the upper meadow
I found a mound of round or nearly round
Rocks a glacier or the tides had ground.
Moss-ringed, lichen-encrusted, water-stained,
They'd lain unmoved since piled there by the hand
That toiled to till this stubborn, stony field.
He harvested its first and heaviest yield
Each year, before he put in beans or corn.
His barrowsfull of turned rocks heaped this cairn
—Not like the cone of stone on Knocknarea
Whose goddess taxes all for tributary
Pebbles placed on the altar that is hers,
Or harrows forgetful pilgrims with her curse;
This rockpile, if at all a monument,
Must be one to the one whose back was bent
And bent again here, though all he stooped to do
Is now, like Troy, as vanished as the dew
Save a pile of rocks where bracken grows.
Were they inscribed, these stones might ask, Who knows
What of his making may, when he is gone,
Bring him, in the viewer's eye, to life again?

At the Lookout

They always start with quick and eager strides
—Even the one on crutches—up the hill.
The long-legged and the young soon reach the bend,
Then reappear above the heads of slower
Earnest pilgrims puffing up the slope.
Those at the parapet stand, statuesque,
Their tiny silhouettes nicking the sky.
See, some now descend the winding trail—
The young, the tall step out, no longer black
And dwarfed against the vast and cloudless light,
Their blouses khaki, red, and white. In single
File, like beads on a string we cannot see,
They reach the stairway to the parking lot,
Then break apart toward different destinations.
Scattered now, does each still hoard some sense
Of borrowed grace from a purpose briefly snatched
And shared beneath the sky, whatever it was?

Quandaries

Why is it, in no way am I the one
I most resemble? Although yesterday
with swivel-headed razor I shaved close,
a stubble thrusts on cheeks and chin;
the cells that are my body, bones, my nerves, my skin
are at this moment dying, self-regenerating, growing, dying,
into the millionth generation since I came
naked, small and bawling from the dark
where everything was found and was O.K.
In their circuits in my brain these cells
can summon what they were not there when sight,
smell, taste, and all the rest inscribed
patterns I at will recall. How come? I walk
out in the garden where the odors
of lilac, sweet alyssum, and viburnum
assail me, each blossom replicating a thousand
thousand thousand earlier blooms. Among
the many questions that have troubled
my waking and disturbed my sleep,
over this I have spent seventy years
in wonder and confusion, but here,
in the garden, I decide
until I'm older, wiser,
to set these quandaries aside.
Now, viburnum, alyssum, lilac mingle,
swathe my senses, and the day is sweet.

Ledges

These raw slabs of rock laid down
in creased oblongs, schists, and squares,
in plateaus, in giants' stairs
with hollows and depressions cupping
pools and puddles from the last high tide,
in one a cautious crab among the barnacles,
another green with primal slime,
while below, the seawall steeply falls
into the bay that stretches toward the distant
sky—a view as desolate as when
these pink-tinged ledges thrust out of the sizzling
sea and cooled, until, at last,
the sun's warmth made mysterious
migrations of dissolved
elements and nutrients combined
in the earliest
self-begotten motions in the world.

Near Tinicum Island

In the shallows near the island
Millroach skitter in the air and water splashing
Like scaled stones.

Free an instant as the skimming birds,
Their sudden glisten gathers
The entirety of the sun,

Then they fall back into the drabber color
Of their accustomed element,
Small fish in a brackish stream.

Some will make it to the sea.

O Pioneers!

As the boy watched
the veins traced a roadmap on the membrane
inside the skin that peeled
back like a rind
slit by knifeblade.
Inside the gash down the belly
guts coiled in their colors.
With gnarled, practiced hands the man detached
pelt from spine, doubling up
one hindleg,
working skin down inside-out
till the foot was inside the fur
and firm red meat of the thigh swelled
within the membrane like a foetus
about to be born. He squeezed
on the cutter, snipped bone
clean at the ankle. Three more
legs to do, then work the pelt over
ears and jaw, taking care, great care
about the eyelids
and nostrils,
the lips.
And now here's skin with little gobs of red meat
still to be scraped, and there's the footless
skinless corpse
all in one piece
except for the loose guts spilling on the table,
looking very helpless indeed.
And, as he said, If you don't want this carcass
I believe I'll cook me some groundhog stew tonight,
the boy looked queasy
yet watched as the knife scraped
little gobs of meat from inside the skin.
He looked at the boy sideways and said,
Now you know what the pioneers
did of an afternoon—

When Dan'l Boone shot a groundhog, or found one
run over by the side of the road, who
do you think skinned and dressed it? and the boy said,
I'd like to be a pioneer some of the time,
But some of the time I wouldn't so much.
By then the windowpane was dark with a sky
the color of bloody bile.
Wrapping the skin and skull in brown paper,
He lit the stove, put his stewpot on, and said he'd clean
the knife and table while his dinner boiled,
and tomorrow the boy can come back to salt the pelt
and peg it out, so when it's dry
he can keep it as long as he lived.
And he did.

Vane

from whichever
direction blowing
the wind spins
its blades causing
the spindle crank to
turn which raises
drops raises the
rod hooked around
a nail in the wooden
woodsman's back so
he bends now stands
now bends his axe
sunk upraised then sunk
into the notch cut
in the log he never
quite chops in
two no matter how
hard blows from
whichever direction
or how long the wind

Going

Your time has come, the yellowed
light of the weary sun
wavers in the foliage.
It's no use, no use to linger.
So, goodbye, day. See,
the shadows join each other
as the air turns shadow
and the light fails. You
are gone, gone into the ghostly
light of all my days, of all
my hungers only partially assuaged,
of all desires
which in the rush of hours
I reached and stooped to grasp.
They're gone, receding like the light,
like the shadows, receding
into subsidence, to come
again as the day comes,
as the night
comes, bringing its own
going in its coming
again, and again.

The Cape Racer

At the auction of the stuff
in the Staples' barn—ox shoes;
the kit for shoeing oxen;
a cider press; an anvil;
a hand-turned clothes washer; the box
of cobbler's lasts and hammers,
nails and rubber heels; a berry rake;
a double-boiler lunch pail
in which the lumberjack's boiled coffee
in the lower pan keeps from freezing
his sandwich in the pan above; a pitchfork;
another pitchfork; a lot of three
hay rakes; and a harness—resisting
all these as the bidders
responded to the auctioneer's
palaver, he an adept
insinuator of desire
in the hard-worked men who stood
under a light rain laughing
at his inevitable joke about
the thundercrock with a cracked
lid somebody bid two bucks for,
I nodded when he lifted and held before us
a Cape racer,

I who didn't need a thundercrock,
harness, hay rakes, lumberman's
lunch pail or cobbler's lasts,
why did I want a Cape racer?
We're never here in winter
when the hill behind the farm is sheeted
with levelled snow and the tall grass
a mere stubble casting long shadows
on the unmarked tilt of crusted meadow,
but I could not resist the lovely shape
of the racer Horace Gray devised and made here

and named for this Cape in '79
of the century before the last, seeing
its length the height of a man
just one inch under six feet long,
its breadth a mere nine inches
—just wide enough to lie on—
the frame, on which the runners,
flat iron bands screwed onto bent ash rods,
support a boy four inches
from the whistling ground,
its twenty-two hand-whittled spars spaced
two inches and a half apart, no thicker
than your little finger, each one fitted
into holes drilled in the sleigh frame's upper bars,
and the racer held together without nails,
rivets, screws, or glue, the thing made taut
by tension of the twisted cords between
the right-hand frame and the left, cords
doubled and turned, turned with a sliver
of wood wedged
between pairs of the spars to hold it fast,
the sleigh so light one hand can hold it
in the air while bids are asked for,
so sleek it seems prepared for flight
over the clouds as well as the frozen hills

—the farmers and the lobstermen,
the lumbermen and berry-rakers
had no need for sleighs, so my initial
nod assenting to the auctioneer's
"Dollarbill, somebody bid me a dollarbill . . ."
has made me owner and proprietor
of a Cape racer I've never raced nor likely
ever shall speed down
the berry field and meadow with the grass tufts slithering
beneath my ears and the cut snow

whipping and stinging
numbed cheeks and reddened knuckles.
It's pleasure enough to see it lean
against the wall all summer,
as ready as ever it was to test
its lightness, strength, and taut design
on the crust of the bright snow or down
the white slope of the mind.

Blizzard

Nothing could stand in the way of its falling.
Day gave up the ghost to silent stormlight,
Like an autumn bear the sun slunk back in its lair.

Comfort and warmth, for those who remembered them,
Were compressed by the huge weight of the present,
Recalled like fossil leaves in stone.

Who could count how long the snow came down
While days were nights and nights were winter?
Time was trapped in the dark, in the icy wind.

Then the shape-shifting wind from the cave of the unseen king
Whose dominion is illusion
Rearranged bulk, expanse, surfaces, height

In the geometry of another country
Where we once had recognized our houses,
Trees, fences, gardens, roads.

When like ferrets we tunnelled out of our burrows
And blinkingly peered around us, dazed
And dazzled by the merciless shine,

On pathless ways through untracked nowhere
We saw relations of mounds and valleys,
Of no known objects in the one uncolor,

As purity poured into our eyeballs, with the pain
Of perfect whiteness where even the shadows
Are less white than white but of a whiteness still.

What could we do to reclaim the unfamiliar
And make it again into images of the familiar
With our clumsy mittened hands?

Yet, in less than a week, the tall drifts scattered
On aimless winds, and then, as the winds died
And rootmounds slowly sank and icicles fell,

Houses, trees, fences appeared again.
Now ruts are runnels, and under snowmelt
On the icy pavement footsteps linger

Of one who when the storm had just begun
Passed unseen and vanished. Now we reclaim
Our shovelled paths and unblocked roads, the shrinking

Snowpiles pocked with dirt. The earth despoils
With slush, soils the snow with sludge. This is our world—
We are earth's people, the earth's smudge is our sign.

2

Fables

What does it matter that the tales are lies,
That a lad like none the villagers had known,
Meeting a poor old man at the crossroads, shares
Half his own crust, not, like both his brothers,
Bidding the beggar with curse and kick begone,

The beggar who fills the boy's noggin with the need to bring
A drop of water from the Well at the World's End home
(Just so as to find what good might come of it),
With no man to point the road to the end of the world
But only Earth, and Sea, and the Sky to send him

Forth to thwart the Crone, the Giant, the Sea-Troll
Who would prevent him, but since his heart is pure
He will be aided—a talking horse befriends him,
A dolphin, and a sparrow with second sight
Reveal the gifts to help his quest perdure,

The stone that will not miss whatever it's thrown at,
The cloak he walks invisible in, the feather
That the winds waft always toward the World's End
Where at last he'll dip his jug in that clear well
And sail for home with a teardrop of its water,

Holy water his good luck brims in, beaching
In a far demesne whose princess he will marry
And take in his craft by winds borne to this village
Where all the folk remember him, and he
Will lead his bride to bed, but first they tarry

And harken, by the embers, to the stories
Of a lad like none the villagers had known,
Who shares his crust with a beggarman so wise
He sends him forth to find his fate alone
—What does it matter that the tales are lies?

The Celtic Twilight, 1965

1. *Dromahair*

A rook-swept abbey scars one hill,
A castle's ruin wounds the other.
In their defile a disused silent mill
Crumbles toward the racing water.

Field of thistle, crop of thorn.
A randy donkey's found the gap
In a fallen fence of stone.
It's on the mare he's mounting up.

And there's the gypsy's cart, his fire,
And swilling a stick in the pot, his crone.
It rains. A chill grips my desire
For all I would disown or own.

2. *Connemara*

Old stones, old thatch.
Speaking Gaelic here
Elders sip beer.
Theirs this harsh parish
Of the ancient tongue
Of an ancient race.
Few of the young
Stick it out in this place.

3. *A Bard*

And what was Austin Clarke's reply when Frost
Asked, "What sort of poems do you write?"
"I climb
Into a jungle gym, then dance"—no boast
From one who knew the burden of a bard
Makes each encounter with his language hard,
Till wrested into form, and wrung in rhyme.

On First Looking into Lattimore's Homer

With smaller Latin and less Greek
Than Keats, I had to roam
With those who rowed on perfumed seas.
My trireme was launched in the Eighteen Nineties,
The wrath of Achilles but a tinted scene
On tapestries
Embroidered, unreal,
In a language none could feel or speak.

Now the seas snarl where an arrogant keel
Supple through swell and spume
Dares tread the god-infested Mediterranean.
See doom-bound Hektor, eager to assuage
Blood-maddened rage—
How we are torn,
Whether to exult or mourn,
Swept on the surge of lines we speak and feel.

Philosophy

In sophomore year the great philosopher,
Then ninety, out of retirement come to pass
His wisdom on to one more generation,
Read his last lecture to our class.

That afternoon, the mote-filled sunlight leaned
Attentively through tall
Windows in amber buttresses that seemed
To gird the heavens so they wouldn't fall.

The blaze of his white mane, his hooded eyes,
The voice that plumbed us from reflection's skies
So far above temptation or reward—

The scene has never left my mind. I wrote
His lecture down, but, in an old trunk, my notes
Have crumbled, and I can't call back a word.

Philosophy of Composition

I'll flog you no more, old horse,
Old brain, weary-hoofed, thirsty,

You can't take me any farther. So lie down here
And wait for my return.

I'll seize power without you.
I'll plunge on

Without a thought into the tangles
Of the hair of stars,

I'll get there without the tedium
Of turning passions

Into thoughts, of turning thoughts
To speech. Feelings will find me,

Words will come, the right ones,
Giving no thought, and taking none.

Violence

After I'd read my poem about a brawl
between two sidewalk hustlers—one,
insulted, throws the other down and nearly
kills him—over coffee and cookies a grave

senior citizen reproved me: *How*
could you see such violence and you
didn't try to stop them? —Oh, I explained,
it wasn't like that, really—I saw

two guys in a shoving match and thought
I'd write about aggression, what
anger really feels like. . . . *Yes,*

and if the one got killed
it would be on your head.
You should've stopped them, he said.

A True Confession

Could I say,
Exalt the primacy of the id, the gonad,
the holiness of Me,
the electric ecstasy of those who go mad,

practice the absolute
freedom of the soul and beard to grow
and screw the resolute
endeavors of the mind to know

anything, because
in this senility of institutions
there are no laws
but beatitudes in the transfixions

of talented creators
who seek in orgiastic nurture
to liberate their meters
from the iamb's Chinese water-torture . . .

or, Could I say,
Ignore your senses, five unfaithful stewards;
the arrogant ego,
fallen on hard times, moves towards

imperfect submission
to perfect laws, and better had admit
its true condition
so grace may yet descend to it;

practice true numbers,
in strictness of the stanza find
the discipline that disencumbers
the featly gestures of a nimble mind—

O, I'd make poems and more poems every day!
One week I'd scan
all the Greek myths in a gospel way
symbolizing Modern Man,

next week, declaim "Epic Me!" out loud,
all guts and gristle in a wallow
of words anarchic as a screaming crowd
dismembering Apollo—

But it's no good. No, I can't violate
my single double nature
and by reduction of myself, create
either half-creature,

not even for a poem's sake
sever nerve-ends from the brain
to think too purely and avoid the ache
of ecstasy, or the throb of pain;

I'd be an undivided man who wields
the contradictions
soul surmises and the cortex feels
to speak in fictions

what truths of love or suffering I find
in forms as fitting
as skill and will and luck combined
may make, all half-unwitting.

3

Saturday

An experiment results in the transmutation
    of a fly and a man. When
the old castle of a vampire baron is restored
    the baron returns and goes
on a killing spree. A mad scientist transplants his
    insane assistant's brain in
another human. After a baby sea-monster
    is captured off the coast of
Ireland and placed in a London circus, its angry
    father makes a shambles of
the city. Suffering from exhaustion, a pop singer
    comes to a bee farm for rest
only to find her life endangered by the insane
    beekeeper. A vampire must
prey upon living humans to sustain its own life.
    The life of a young woman
is irrevocably changed when she moves into a
    sinister house. A public
opinion analyst, stumbling on a hillbilly
    family, becomes involved
in murder. A successful songwriter decides to
    pursue the girl of his dreams.

The Gift of Tongues

I the Scop of my own Saga
You the Epic Hero of your Epic
She the Lady of her Sonnet Sequence
—What will become of us

Now all the forms are broken,
Jibberjabber written, spoken,
Automation causing traffic jams?
Virtual employment bursts the till

In the Shop-'N'-Save.
America really moves the goods,
America's got the goods. Nothing's for free.
Who needs the gift of tongues?

Speech

It's hard to tell which
of his cluckings and gnashings
are consonants for sure.
Not easy, though you try

to make out his vowels
from the slurps, to distinguish
among noises, words.
But the fellow wants to communicate,

he has things on his mind to say.
So wherever he goes he carries
an alphabet on a folding board.
You'd think it was chess or backgammon,

and if he'd sit still for a minute
and keep his head from lolling
it would seem he is wild about games.
He has stumbled onto the bus,

he's sprawled in an empty seat.
Now he points a twisted finger
to one, then another letter.
The woman beside him looks around her.

He thrusts the board before her.
His limbs have lives of their own.
Should she move to another seat?
Strange gurgles come out of his throat.

Everyone's looking at her.
Why does he want her to look
as his forefinger gropes toward the J?
Of what is it that she is afraid?

Now his finger crawls back to the box
containing the E, and stops,
She watches it lunge to the S
while the skin around his mouth

stretches in sideways smile.
His thumb seems screwed on backwards
but the forefinger jerks back and forth
as she sits perfectly still

to U and returns to S
and lurches away and returns
to S and the woman beside him
has all this while been bemused

to know what he was doing.
But that's not the problem now.
She can guess what he's trying to say
but not what she should reply,

or how to address a creature
in such a case—should she speak
with especially slow
and clear enunciation

so he could read her lips?
She knows she has only the time
he takes to fumble and find
the A, the V, then E

and S to make up her mind.
Later she will recall
she wasn't afraid at all.
It was like talking to someone

who is wearing a strange disguise. "Yes,
that's true"—her words once out,
his body for a time is still
as is one who is eased of his burden.

Mean Street

In sneaks, in shorts, in tie-dyed tee-shirts,
one burly, blond, the other swarthy,
leaner, younger, snatch at each other
circling, till one gets an armlock
on the other's head. A pretty hot day for
fooling around with Greco-Roman,
or is it Catch-as-Catch-Can?—only
they're not fooling. They edge each other
grimly within the ring of onlookers
each trying to throw the other off
balance, enormous effort—the lean one
shoves his knee between the other's
legs and down they fall, hard
on the cracked pavement, scattering tattered
piles of magazines, the plastic
sunglasses with sequins or without,
each merchandise displayed on two
squares of pavement precisely, as though
by treaty, jumbled as the blond guy
lands on his back in grime, trying
to arch his back, to turn, but the lean one
prevents and pinions him, then grasps
a fistful of his long hair and beats
the back of his head on the pavement, a *thud*
and a *thud,* a *thud*— If y'ever call
me that again—a *thud*—I'll KILL ya,
d'ya hear? his flushed tiger face
glares, fangs bared. On his back
the blond guy looks scared, feebly
surrenders. He's had it. The insulted feels
the insult, whatever it was, was not
worth really killing the bastard
—though it feels good, good, the power
to do it, calm with surely knowing
a couple or three more *thuds*—so easy!—
and the guy'd be dead. So, can it

satisfy, letting him off with
just the pain, the fear, and then
remembering the fear, the pain?
Still holds his hair, could give a quick
yank, a real *thud* . . . But no,
he'll be content, this time, to gloat
on the other's fear, his pain, his shame.
They separate, get up, dust off,
the loser gazing far away,
the victor staring through him while
the passersby who'd stopped their passing
to form the ring that made this brawl
a gladiator's struggle break
and melt away. A couple stay
to help re-establish peace,
gathering the sunshades flung
or kicked into the gutter, stacking
the magazines in rows again.
Grimly, the merchants mind their wares.
They've made no sales. The people fade.
A taut, baneful silence reigns.

A Sidewalk Scene

It's a *modus vivendi* of sorts, not dying
on a heap of rags and a dirty blanket, lying
beneath a plastic sheet and three umbrellas,
handles linked with string, their ribs a trellis
just above the head shielded from rain
while *sotto voce* carrying on again
half a dialogue, tracing in air
an impatient or expressive gesture,
now dropping filthy fingers from a face
wrinkled as the map of Iceland, toothless,
mumbling a reply to someone else
not there to hear her catalogue of ills
as back and forth she's rocking, back and forth,
back and forth, as one who by the hearth
holds an infant, or is an infant held.
The passers pass her by, their steps unstilled
by the *tableau vivant* acted before them;
swaddled in her spell, she can ignore them
who stroll untouched by how her life has withered
or what she might have been before she gathered
umbrellas, rags on the sidewalk, there to huddle,
daft old woman, an unwitting sibyl
in a city where compassion's stricken numb,
as though its prophecy of things to come.

Ballad of the Day

Was it yesterday or was today the day
when the raven drank slow tears
that tolled the curfew, and the shadow writing
on the plain of snow?

Was the day another yesterday when singing
black upon the gibbet, raven flew
from the crematories, drunk
on the smoke and writing

the deaths of brothers on the snow?

Never! they reply— The smoke
never wrote the black
song of drunken raven
on the plain. Never, neither

yesterday, nor other yesterday!
Do you hear the cry that cleaves
slow tears of the bell
tolling the brothers' deaths? O, No,

they answer, No, it is the shadow
of the evening writes across the plain
smudge on snow
the hour, as always.

[from the Italian of Ruth Domino]

A Riddle

If all but one deny me, I am not.
The Greeks had gods for everything but me.
                                                            Since then
How could I live on earth, in heaven? Yet see
If you can find me in the hearts of men.

[Peace]

4

Emblems

When the mandibles of the clock have gnawed
The journal of another day,
So many drawn breaths nearer
A next incarnation,

I find in that no solace.
My enterprise dissembles nature's plan.
I would hold age in stiff abeyance
And command time's watchdog to obedience

To the intensities of joy: A windy
Cloudless day of dolphins around a dory
Beachfire, the surge, the wildness of the sea,

And the secret fissures of one woman's love
—Among the emblems I array to daunt
Too swift precessions of the moon and sun.

Heartbreak

Delicate delicate delicate
The workings of a soul,
Captive lucent creature
In its box of bone,
How easily wounded by the stroke
It must endure alone—

Difficult difficult difficult
The soul's attempt to sing
That was made for song. The single
Soul's but half a choir
Inchoate until wedded
In accord with its desire

Desire desire the double
Of the self that seeks
Imaginable completion
—Harmonious perfection!
If once thought found, then lost,
How make sound the chord that breaks?

Devotion

To carve this long-haired, melon-breasted girl,
His blade caressing every curve and curl
Of her slim hips and coiled, voluptuous tail,
Her lover had to slay, then flay, a whale.

Scott Nearing's Ninety-Eighth Year

Shsh, Zzzzz; Shh, Zzzzz:
from behind the stone house the hissing
of the bucksaw's blade in rhythm
as though the day is drawing breath—

there, at a sawhorse between two rows of cordwood
stacked five feet high and longer than the house is,
he, at ninety-seven, is sawing, sawing
a twisted gnarl of maple

—of course I grab the other end and pull.
He pulls, I pull, he pulls, and the teeth
sizzle, sizzle, as the crack spits
white sawdust to the ground, until

we have to turn the knotted chunk, so heavy
it nearly topples from the sawhorse, to change
our angle of attack. Scott grasps a wedge,
slips it in the crevice, taps it

with a maul. No go. He knocks it out
and now we saw again. I'm in a sweat,
this day is hotter than I'd thought.
On either side of us stand wagonloads

of well-split cordwood. Why are we toiling, toiling
to cut into stove-sized logs a recalcitrant
knot—has this old man spent all his life
gnawing intractable problems, so can't now stop?

"When we've finally cut this thing in pieces
small enough to fit into your stove,
how much warmer will it make your house?" I asked,
as he pulled, and I pulled, and he pulled the saw.

"That's not the question," he said, sliding
the bucksaw free, then slipping in the wedge again.
"Each stroke" (*tap-tap*) "is a lengthening" (*tap-tap*)
"of life"—as the gnarl split and the wedge clanged

on the ground. Now Helen calls me to come in and see
how the last book she's written begets another book,
while Scott puts bucksaw, maul, and wedge away
in each appointed place. In the Franklin stove

a log smoulders. He lifts a yard-long tube,
breathes on the sullen embers—red,
yellow flames dance, spread feathers from the ash
arising from their last night's fire.

Revisiting the Country of His Youth

How will he repossess what memory
Has held so long and kept intense for him?
—Stride confidently forth, an amputee
On phantom limb

Bob

Hadn't been out of the house, except
once a week to the hospital, since
that day three months ago when they brought him
home from the mine, doubled over
in pain, no longer breathing acid fumes
or dust from the schists the copper ran in,
but sick, sick inside. So I didn't expect
while scraping and sanding my hourglass puller
tipped keel-up above the tide-line
to see come, slowly down the hill
to the beach road, his big green pickup
with the front hitch for a snowplow and movable
spotlights on the cab, and him
driving. He stopped, rolled the window down,
looked out and said, Be sure you caulk
those seams around the keel. Beside him
Katherine gave a wan smile. Then, toward us
came that little red Toyota
of Hobie's, who'd had hard words from him
two winters past about cutting wrongside
of the line between their woodlots. Since then
they hadn't spoken, but Hobie stopped,
leaned from his window and called out, Hey there!
Good to see ya!! D'ya know the mackerel
are running? My boy hauled in a bucketful
at the town wharf last night. And next
Bing's empty dump truck roared and rattled
across the beach, then stopped, blocking
the road—Hiya (as though they'd spoken
only the day before)—We've finished
roofing that house on Varnumville
—talk whittled down to the dailiness
of living and the expectation of
tomorrow. I said, If you don't stop by,
Liz will be disappointed. So I got in
beside them. He winced, putting the truck

in gear. It rolled up to our drive.
At the table by the window we watched
the cove's arms embrace sun-deckled water
stirred by cat's-paw breezes as the gulls
swooped and terns dove. You can see
thirteen islands, he said, from here
(and, as his father had done for us
a quarter-century before, he called
their roll)—Pond Isle, and Beach,
Butter, Colt's Head, Horse's Head, North Haven,
Eagle Isle, Western, and Resolution . . . He said
the names as one who tolls his beads
before leaving on a long journey
so that never would he forget
this place, these islands,
wherever it is that he'll be gone.

A Time Piece

When, after much shaking, my watch,
its stem stuck fast, refused to go, the tide

ceased scrambling up the pebbled beach,
the moon three-quarters full stared still

from the same unmoving rafter of the sky,
and a lone bird launched its melancholy

call, o, o, the single note
a plangent echo of itself, then I,

born into change, thought such a stoppage
can only be the grip of death—but how

can this be death, since I am seeing nothing
that changes and all that does not change,

feeling the thump, the double thump of heartbeats,
or is it the same beat beating again,

again, again, again, again? If this is
the way death is, it keeps a body

from ever growing older while the future
pours through each evanescent moment, and

before we'd savored it, becomes
the past, but freed from that relentless progress

I've freedom to do nothing but get used
to being the way we now forever are,

no chance to choose another president,
prices fixed at last night's last quotations

until the very end of time since this
is the end of time, and now no

grudges can be healed, no injuries
forgiven nor friendships made, and nothing

can be done for love, nothing shared
or sacrificed, love cannot ripen, deepen,

staying as it now is, uncompleted
while the heart grows slowly rigid, colder,

void as space between the stars. Is there
no escape from feeling nothing? I shake

my watch, I shake it—*clicka! clicka!*—bands
release the hands that swing now clockwise down

the dial—ripples roil the shore, the moon
swings on its arc, and as the sky pales

a forestful of choristers sing, tweedle,
cry *Today's alive, alive, alive!*

How fast the time that time stopped on my wrist
has passed, and fading, dwindles in the past.

A Resurrection

When I arose I knew I had been dead.
My fingers and my lungs still gray with clay,
Before my eyes a gleaming world unrolled.
Behind, the dark curled deeper in its cell.

What cold grip clutched my back? Moldy breath
At each gulp clearer, warmer . . . I am forgetting
The long impenetrableness of death
Beyond remembrance and past all forgetting.

Coffee! OJ! Let this day be a boon!
In clarifying light, in freshening weather
Memory revives—the future is its gift

While shadows of tall clocks shrivel in the sun.
I'll plunge into the maelstrom of our swift
Redemptive life, for there may be no other.

Who We Are

On a morning like this one, when the mist is lit from within,
a silvery light without center that envelops you so that you breathe
light in the air and you can't even see to the mailbox, it's then
you feel cut off from time, dangling in space suspended: Where
in this silvery glow are the deeds, the chants, the annals, the tales
of the Founders of Cities, the Heroes who saved us from past
allegorical monsters, historical perils, from real dangers imagined
and imaginary dangers made real by being
predicted after the fact by poet and oracle? It was
these—the strophes that told how Grandfather's own great-grandfather,
with only his own shrewd courage and motherwit, broke
the back of the wind and manacled wrists of the waves,
by guise and disguise outwitting the one-eyed warrior-shaman
who led the horde that surrounded our palisade (Remember
how his captive Raven leapt on the enemy's head, black
wings blindfolding the chieftain's eye while the great beak croaked
its doomward prophecy, routing
all terrified outlanders!)—it was these,
as we coped each day with a new raw dawn, a further
spilling of the sun in the roiling sea, that made us aware
of who we are and in that knowing
felt resurgent the ancient strengths of night and early day. Nothing
there was in our world that denied us this: The brickwork city,
the wooden sills, the clay rooftiles, the gables, steeples, the pewter
mugs, stoneware jugs, the cobbled streets, toward evening
the reaching shadows, all, all were what they were, none threatened
the clock with a sundial's obsolescence where the garden fountain
is perpetually lit by light that has no need to heed
where our tiny sun and insignificant speck of moon may chance
to float in their cubit of space around this dustfleck
we do our dreams on. Now, if we could see
through the globuled light like a featureless movie screen
with only the projector's bulb intensified before the flicker
of coming attractions disturbs and distorts the blazing white
monochrome of its purity, we could find

what denies us this. Denies
by the hum and clatter that rise not with the wind nor fall as the wind fades,
denies by the clutter of junked vehicles encircling earth in rings
parodic of those other planets' moons, denies by thrusting, swollen shadow
of mushroom clouds that billow above the wind and drop their wizard's curses
on distant pasturage, on heads of newborn babes. Denies
the place of our space, denies the time
of our time gone before, expanse of time
stretching as a prairie on which the first covered wagon had but travelled
the first few leagues while ahead there beckoned
undulant plain, the rumbling bison herds, a vivid sky
streaked with circling hawk and eagle, now shrunken out of mind
behind the gilded arches of our miracle miles, our
car lots, parking lots, developed lots, the neon arms
arching over asphalt so that night shall never fall.
The fourteen screens in the show window all are tuned
to the same minuscule mannikin in unison enacting
the same holdup firing the same shot driving the getaway car in wild evasion
of the same pursuit crashing the same barrier amid the same
crescendo of squealing tires and the same
interruptions announcing the virtues of the same
floor cleaner. Now
will your lines recall
our vanished world as far behind us now as
Achilles' vengeance was and the heaped dead and blackened stumps
of Troy's walls fallen in twilight were to those Achaean towns
that required a blind man's lyre to keep them from forgetting,
or will your lines take shape from the shapelessness around you,
the jointed facts devoid of nature where our hive
pursues and still pursues our ends
unknown while stars still hold their posts in beleaguered constellations,

and still the planets swing in accustomed arcs around us, and the earth
ignorant of our quick profits and brief pleasures, as before
drinks rain, hoards its green force through seasons of ice, of deprivation,
till it feed roots again, offers its annual bounty to the fecund, the lucky
fields of daisies, the woodchuck in the bank, the treetop cicada
who, living in time's terrain and in the rhythms
of space, of space and time know nothing.

Called Back

It's got to be a big one, so resonant
is its repeated cry—the sound of a cracked
bronze bell twice struck under water
—so it's not a bittern ('a slow, deep
ong-ka-choonk, ong-ka-choonk'), nor a Great
Blue Heron ('Deep harsh croaks: *frahnk, frahnk,*
frahnk') that keeps on throbbing in the twilight,
in deepening dark, till, in thick woods, sounding
closer now, the insistent, endlessly
repeated call—through the fringe of tall spruce
at the field's edge I with fox-tread walk, thrust
onward toward the bird's reclusive summons,
seeming nearer, by black boughs concealed now,
then farther off, in deeper, darker woods,
so I press through the warm and moist black air
at once so menacing, yet half-familiar
as though, sometime, before remembering,
I'd been here and the two-toned urgent throbbing
in my ears, my arms, my chest, was all
that I could hear in all-encroaching blackness
till from that impenetrable murk I burst
free, in a clearing, rock-crags under sky!
I climb the cairn at the center of this field
at the center of the forest—there, above
Orion's shoulders, the whole vast turning sky
alight with planets, constellations, stars,
a silky wash of dots banding the heavens
where, as I watch, light from the faintest,
farthest sources mingles with the flecks
from nearer stars, and closer still the sudden
streaking meteors, the Perseids showering
lines of light that fade as soon as seen,
—Time made visible as space, contained
in my stunned gaze that holds at once
the end and the beginning and the black
blankness of the unlit nothing that precedes
the first, the earliest, the oldest light.

A Witness

When asked by Friends to speak of poetry
what could I say?
It did seem preordained
in the only house of worship in the Commonwealth
named for a poet, that I read
Winfield Scott's noble colloquial poem,
"It is easier to forget than to have been
Mr. Whittier . . ." How different
from the homely rhetoric of Whittier,
yet probity of discourse as of purpose
and the feeling so much finer
than any of the words.
Quakers, in song, sing Whittier's words,
praying, wring the tongue with silence—
no words, or few.
In the spare meetinghouse
in the quietest beseeching,
the only ornament involuntary rainbows
where from a cracked pane wintry light
leapt, broken
colors vivid on a wall of white,
with heads bowed,
the world renounced as long as stillness
echoed in the room,
Friends prayed. We felt the silence
swell with concentrated purpose,
syllables of thought
in questioning, in waiting,
and the light shift
clearer a little.